IDITAROD DREAM

Dusty and His Sled Dogs Compete in Alaska's Jr. Iditarod

TED WOOD

Walker and Company
New York

First published in the United States of America in 1996 by Walker Publishing Company, Inc.

Published simultaneously in Canada by Thomas Allen & Son Canada, Limited, Markham, Ontario

Library of Congress Cataloging-in-Publication Data
Wood, Ted.
Iditarod dream: Dusty and his sled dogs compete in Alaska's Jr. Iditarod / Ted Wood.
p.   cm.
Summary: Relates the story of the fifteen-year-old Alaska boy and his dogs as they prepare for and then run the 158-mile course of the Jr. Iditarod Race.
ISBN 0-8027-8406-2 (hardcover). —ISBN 0-8027-8407-0 (reinforced)
1. Whittemore, Dusty—Juvenile literature. 2. Jr. Iditarod Trail Sled Dog Race, Alaska—Juvenile literature.
3. Mushers—Alaska—Biography—Juvenile literature. [1. Whittemore, Dusty. 2. Mushers.
3. Jr. Iditarod Trail Sled Dog Race, Alaska.]
I. Title.
SF440.15.W47W66 1996
798'.8—dc20   95-31084
                                                                                CIP
                                                                                AC

Book design by Chin-Yee Lai
Map on page 4 by Dennis O'Brien
Photo page 33 © Ted Levin, Animals Animals/Earth Scenes

Printed in Hong Kong
2 4 6 8 10 9 7 5 3 1

To all the young mushers who keep the great tradition of sled-dog racing alive.

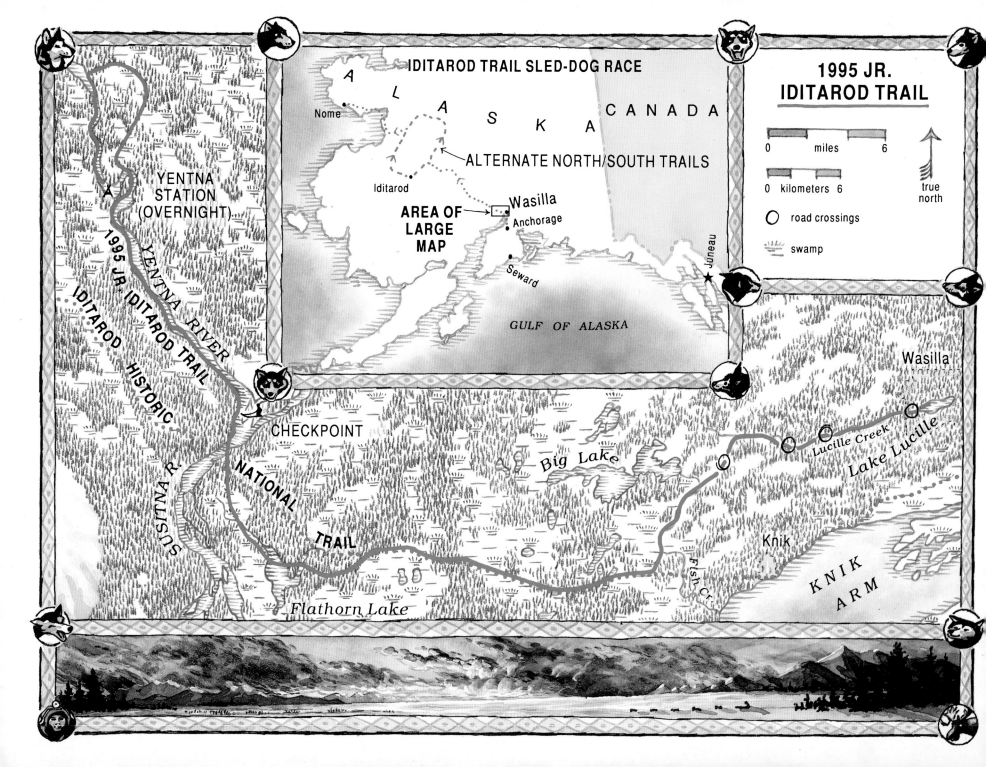

1995 JR. IDITAROD TRAIL

IDITAROD TRAIL SLED-DOG RACE

A L A S K A

CANADA

Nome

ALTERNATE NORTH/SOUTH TRAILS

Iditarod

Wasilla

AREA OF LARGE MAP

Anchorage

Seward

Juneau

GULF OF ALASKA

0 miles 6

0 kilometers 6

true north

○ road crossings

swamp

YENTNA STATION (OVERNIGHT)

1995 JR. IDITAROD TRAIL

YENTNA RIVER

IDITAROD HISTORIC

SUSITNA R.

NATIONAL TRAIL

CHECKPOINT

Flathorn Lake

Big Lake

Wasilla

Lucille Creek

Lake Lucille

Knik

Fish Cr.

KNIK ARM

Each March, as the darkness of winter begins to fade, an excitement spreads across Alaska. With the daylight comes Alaska's most famous event—the Iditarod Trail Sled-Dog Race. Known as the last great race, the Iditarod pits musher and dog against nature's most severe conditions. Starting in Anchorage, the racers drive their teams over mountain passes, through bitter Arctic winds, and across frozen seas to Nome, 1,180 miles away.

But dog mushing wasn't always a sport in Alaska. Eskimos in the Far North used their huskies for work, pulling their hunting sleds across the ice in search of seals. In winter, towns like Nome were cut off from the rest of Alaska as sea ice blocked the ports. Mail and supplies had to come from Anchorage by sled, pulled by the same Eskimo huskies.

In the winter of 1925, Nome was hit with a horrible epidemic: diphtheria. There was no medicine in town—and without medicine, everyone might die. The race was on to save the town. A dog team sped from Anchorage, carrying the life-saving medicine, which was relayed team to team all the way to Nome. The brave mushers and dogs succeeded. The medicine stopped the epidemic and saved Nome.

Dog teams no longer supply Nome. Snowmobiles and airplanes now connect the town to southern Alaska. But the heroism of the dog teams was not to be forgotten, and in 1973 a famous Alaskan musher named Joe Redington decided to honor their bravery with a race that followed the same trail as the medicine relay to Nome. The trail was the Iditarod, and the race was named for the trail.

Because the race was so difficult and dangerous, only adults could enter. There was no event for young mushers dreaming of an Iditarod championship. So in 1977, race organizers started the Jr. Iditarod for kids fourteen to seventeen years old. Starting in the town of Wasilla, just north of Anchorage, the two-day race follows a portion of the Iditarod National Trail. The dog teams run to an overnight camp and back, finishing in Wasilla 158 miles later. This is the story of the Jr. Iditarod and of a young musher whose winning spirit leads him to victory.

Introduction

In Cantwell, Alaska, the February sun barely peeks over the surrounding mountains as fifteen-year-old Dusty Whittemore gets ready for school. Outside, it's thirty degrees below zero, but Dusty is used to it. He's spent his whole life in rugged central Alaska, at first living in an old school bus with his parents and ten sled dogs, then moving to the small log cabin where seventeen dogs now share the front yard.

Before leaving, Dusty says good morning to his most experienced sled dog,
Ozone, who is injured and now sleeps in
the warm kitchen. As he leaves the wood-
heated house, a blast of bitter air freezes
his nylon warm-ups. They make crackling
sounds as he slips quietly through the
sleeping dogs in their little houses. Luckily,
Dusty doesn't have far to walk in this cold.
The Cantwell School is just down the
street. Dusty's in tenth grade and he's been
going to this school since kindergarten.

As in many schools in the Alaska bush where there aren't many students, all the grades share just a few classrooms. In the whole Cantwell School, there are only twenty-seven students and three teachers. Some classes don't even have live teachers. Instead, a television links the students to a teacher elsewhere in the state.

The high school has six students, and Dusty is the only boy. Today, he's having a hard time concentrating on school. His five classmates tease him about this weekend's sled-dog race, the Jr. Iditarod.

Dusty hurries home from school for his last training run before the race. As he comes into the yard, the dogs spin in excited circles and jump up and down on their houses. The dogs live outside, but even though it's fifteen degrees below zero they aren't cold. Alaskan huskies are adapted to the cold and have two layers of fur to keep them warm.

Dusty says hello to them all and gives his lead dog Annie a big nuzzle. The dogs are not pets to the Whittemores; they are working athletes. Some people believe that it's wrong to turn dogs into racers, that it's abusive to make them run. But sled dogs love to run, and the Whittemores treat their dogs like family members. Most important, they are Dusty's loyal friends and will run their hearts out for him.

Dusty and his father load the dogs into tiny cubbyholes in the truck. Each dog has its own little traveling compartment. Usually, the dogs pull the sled right from the house. But now there's a frozen river to cross, and the dogs could slip and injure a leg or be dragged by the rest of the team across the ice. Dusty is too nervous to risk this. The last run before a race is always scary for him. He doesn't want to press his luck.

The dogs can't wait to get on the trail, and as Dusty and his dad hook them up to the pull lines, they yip and howl and jump straight up in the air. Dusty trains with the same ten dogs he'll race with. They run side by side in pairs. The first two are called the lead dogs. They are usually the smartest and most experienced. They have to know how to follow the trail and obey the commands Dusty yells from the sled.

When they're ready to go, Dusty pulls out the big metal safety hook holding the sled back and yells, "Annie, QT!" His two lead dogs hear their names and take off like a shot. The fourteen-mile trail winds through tiny wind-beaten trees and up onto a vast plateau surrounded by mountains. Big deerlike animals called caribou spend the winter here; they watch as Dusty and the dogs speed by.

The trail is very rough, and Dusty has to use all his skills to keep the sled from hitting a tree or tipping over. When he yells "Gee!" Annie and QT turn right. "Haw" turns them left and "Whoa" stops them. "Come gee" or "Come haw" turns the dogs 180 degrees right or left.

Dusty sighs with relief when they finish the course. The last run is over, and the dogs are in the best condition he's ever seen. They've trained three days a week on this loop, and on the weekends they've run 50-mile trails. In summer, when there wasn't snow, the dogs trained by pulling Dusty on an all-terrain vehicle down the highway.

After Dusty and his father feed the dogs, it's time to tune his sled. Like the sleds used by the Eskimos, Dusty's is made from curved, flexible wood and is over eight feet long. His first sled, which he got when he was six, was only a few feet long and was pulled by one dog. His next was a three-dog sled, and now his racing sled is pulled by ten dogs. The more dogs you have, the longer the sled has to be to handle the speed and power of the larger team.

Dusty follows his father's suggestions as he checks the foot brake and the ribbed rubber mat he stands on between the runners to slow the sled down. Together they put fast new plastic bottoms on the sled's runners. Dusty has learned everything he knows about mushing from his father, who's raced the big Iditarod nine times. His father coached him

through his training and now runs down the checklist of gear Dusty is required to carry. They gather all the lines and ties for the dogs, eighty booties to protect the dogs' feet from rough snow, one headlamp, snowshoes, an ax, twenty pounds of dog food, a stove, matches, a sleeping bag, and extra clothing.

Early the next morning, Dusty and his father load his sled onto the truck and put the dogs into their traveling pens. Ozone, unable to race, watches the truck leave the yard, wishing she were going.

The day is clear and cold. Mount McKinley, the highest peak in North America, stands like a giant before the truck. The trip south to race head-quarters in Wasilla takes four hours.

Dusty's thoughts return to last year's Jr. Iditarod, his first. He remembers the thirty-below-zero temperatures and how his glasses were so coated with ice he couldn't see the trail. And how on the return—when perhaps he'd been headed for victory—he got lost, wandering for four hours before he found the right trail. He finished fourth. But this year his glasses are gone, replaced with contact lenses, and his dog team is the best he's ever had. He can only hope the huskies take him down the right trail.

That evening they reach Iditarod headquarters, where all the racers are gathered for the pre-race meeting. He sees familiar faces from last year—Andy Willis, the favorite to win this year, and Noah Burmeister, who came all the way from Nome. One at a time the fifteen racers pick numbers from a hat to set their starting positions in tomorrow's race. (There is no number 1 position competing in the race; instead the slot is reserved to honor a dedicated supporter of that year's Jr. Iditarod race.) The racers start two minutes apart. Dusty picks number 6, a good position and the same he had last year. Andy will start fourteenth and Noah ninth. Dusty leaves with his father for his final night's sleep before the race.

The next morning Dusty and his dad arrive two hours before the race. It's zero degrees, which is perfect for the dogs. Any warmer, and they would overheat. The race begins on frozen Lake Lucille and runs seventy-nine miles north through forests, over windswept swamps, and up the ice-covered Yentna River to a cabin called Yentna Station, the halfway point.

Last year the race started ten miles farther up the trail. Dusty is worried about starting here. The lake ice is barely covered with snow and is so hard that if he loses control at the start, he could get dragged across the lake. His safety hook, used to stop and hold the sled, won't be able to grab the ice. Dusty checks the brakes on his sled and begins to pack the required supplies. Every racer must carry two pounds of food per dog in case of emergency, and must finish with the same amount. (The four pounds each dog will eat for dinner has been flown to Yentna Station the day before.)

Ten minutes before his start, Dusty, his father, and three friends working as handlers hook the dogs up to the sled. Each dog looks small but is tremendously powerful. Dusty has to walk each dog from the truck, lifting its front legs off the snow. With all four legs down, a sled dog would pull Dusty off his feet. Even hooked up, the dogs are so excited by the other teams it takes every hand to hold them in place.

Dusty's team moves to the starting line, straining against the handlers. His mother rides the sled with him, stepping on the brakes to help control the sled. She's nervous, remembering how Dusty got lost last time. But she's also very proud, and she kisses him good-bye before hopping off the sled.

The dogs are pulling so hard now that five people can barely hold them back. Then the announcer yells, "Go!" The handlers step away and Dusty flies from the start.

They cross the lake safely, following the red plastic cones marking the route. But as they enter the woods Dusty is on edge. He's never done this part of the trail, and it's crowded with obstacles. Snowmobiles roar along the same trail, and within ten miles he has to cross four roads. Sometimes the roads are so slick the dogs fall, or they get confused by the cars and spectators. Dusty knows he just needs to survive this part until he hits the main Iditarod trail.

At the first road, the team roars over the pavement and around a sharp turn coming off the road. But they're going too fast, and the sled skids sideways, crashing into a tree. Dusty stops dead and can't believe he didn't break the sled. *I'm out of control*, he says to himself. *I'd better slow the team down.*

Back on the trail, he uses his track brake to slow the dogs. He gets them into a strong, steady pace and is able to pass two racers only five miles from the start. He crosses the next road and quickly overtakes another racer. Right before the final road crossing, ten miles out, Dusty passes the last racer. He knows he's in the lead now, that his team is running well, but he can't think about that. He just wants to get through this part and onto the main Iditarod Trail, which he knows from last year's race.

Finally, eleven miles out, Dusty hits the familiar trail leading into the thick Alaskan forest. The team is running perfectly now, strong and fast, as they head into the hilly section of the race. Dusty is in a rhythm, too. He runs beside the sled up hills to lighten the load for his team. Around tight corners he jumps from left runner to right runner, digging in the edges to steer the sled through the curves.

The trail is only a few feet wide in the woods, and coming around a blind corner the dogs run smack into two snowmobiles stopped in the path. Unable to pass, the dogs spin and run in circles, tangling their lines before Dusty can get to them. It takes him five minutes to straighten them out and get under way. As he goes around the next curve and down a hill, he spots another snowmobile roaring full speed toward him. The machine almost hits Annie and QT in the lead, but it flies off the trail to avoid the collision. The two lead dogs stop dead, but the

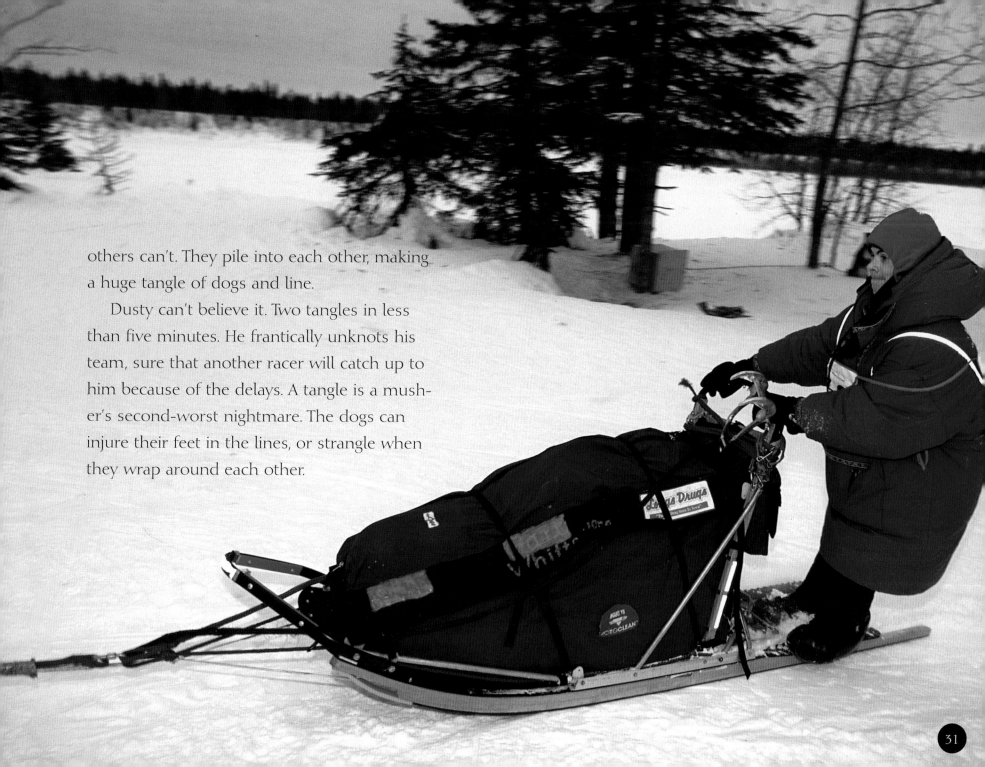

others can't. They pile into each other, making a huge tangle of dogs and line.

Dusty can't believe it. Two tangles in less than five minutes. He frantically unknots his team, sure that another racer will catch up to him because of the delays. A tangle is a musher's second-worst nightmare. The dogs can injure their feet in the lines, or strangle when they wrap around each other.

Finally under way, Dusty and the dogs are on edge and can't settle into a pace. *Please don't see another snowmobile*, he says to himself. Then he spots moose tracks on the trail, and his fears mushroom. Running into a moose is a musher's worst nightmare. Because dogs look like wolves to a moose, a moose may attack a team and can kill several dogs before a musher can frighten it off. There's no going around a moose. If Dusty sees one, all he can do is wait for it to move and hope it doesn't charge.

But the team carries him safely out of the forest and onto a wide, open meadow. Dusty passes a small wooden sign that says "Nome 1,049 miles" and knows from the year before that he can relax for a while through these barren flats. The flats lead to frozen Flathorn Lake, three and a half hours from the start. Here, on the edge of the lake, Dusty takes his first break. He tosses all the dogs fish snacks, big chunks of frozen salmon that will keep their energy up. He says hi to each as well, checking their feet for injuries. QT and Blacky have splits in the webs between their toes, so Dusty puts booties on their feet to protect them as they run.

He takes only five minutes, still expecting to see another racer coming close behind. Trails cross in every direction at the lake, and it's here that Dusty got lost last year. Today, he chooses the right path and speeds out onto the huge snowy lake. It's like running on an ocean of white; Dusty feels relaxed and at home. Out on the lake he suddenly realizes how big his lead is. He can see five miles behind him and there's not one racer in sight. He can't believe it. *Where are Andy and Noah?* he asks himself.

From the lake Dusty turns on to the Susitna River. It looks like a winding snow highway disappearing into the wilderness. Here, he stops at the one checkpoint in the race, and while an official examines his sled and required cargo, Dusty checks the dogs. He decides to take Annie off the lead. She's been looking back while running and seems nervous. She must not have recovered from the encounter with the snowmobile, Dusty thinks.

Dusty moves young Jazz to lead with QT. But Jazz proves too inexperienced, and three miles from the checkpoint Dusty switches Jazz for Bettie. Now the team is running well again, and they move quickly, silently, up a tributary of the Susitna called the Yentna River. There's no need to yell orders here. They know the way to Yentna Station, but Dusty still calls their names to keep them happy.

Just after five P.M.—seven hours after he started—Dusty arrives at Yentna Station, the halfway point and overnight stop. The station is a little log house that can only be reached by plane, snowmobile, or dog sled. Visitors can stay in the house, but racers can't. By the rules, they have to stay with the dogs.

Dusty feels great. He knows he's had a fast race—but, more important, the dogs look fresh and are still eager to run. He smiles to himself, knowing that his training has paid off.

But there's no time to relax. He has hours of dog chores to do. Each racer gets one bale of straw for bedding; after Dusty ties the sled off to a small tree, he spreads the straw around the dogs. It will protect them from the cold snow as they sleep.

Next, he fires up his stove to melt snow for water. While it heats, he fills a cooler with twenty pounds of hamburger and dry food. He pours the heated water into the cooler, letting the frozen meat soak up the warm liquid. Twenty hungry eyes watch as Dusty finally dishes up the warm meal.

After dinner, Dusty checks the dogs' feet for web cracks, putting on ointment where needed. Then he hears other dogs and looks up. He'd forgotten about the other racers. It's Noah, the second racer to arrive at Yentna—thirty-eight minutes behind Dusty. Andy arrives next, eight minutes after Noah. Over the next four hours the remaining racers straggle in. Everyone is required to stay at Yentna ten hours. Dusty arrived so early that his departure time is three-thirty the next morning. He decides not to sleep and helps the other racers build a big fire in the snow. They all help each other; that's the rule of the wilderness.

Before his three-thirty start, Dusty melts more water for the dogs, feeds everyone, packs his sled, and finally makes sure his head-lamp batteries work for the trip back.

It's snowing lightly as he leaves Yentna, and there's no moon. The only light comes from Dusty's headlamp. The dogs are excited to run, but Dusty doesn't like the night. He can't see the trail markers or nearby moose. The dogs are his only eyes, so he chooses Bettie and QT to lead him out. They did the trail once, Dusty figures, so they can do it again.

Once again the dogs are gobbling up the miles. They run the Yentna River and Flathorn Lake in the dark; at first light, Dusty stops at the Nome sign. As he gives the dogs fish snacks, he finally lets himself believe that if nothing bad happens he can expect to win. Dusty and his team move through the hills easily and take all four road crossings smoothly.

Finally, the lake appears, like a welcome mat, and Dusty begins to smile as he heads for the finish. He's running so fast that the spectators and most of the racers' families haven't arrived yet. But he spots his mother and father cheering him on, and when he crosses the finish line his mother showers him with hugs and kisses. His father's proud smile is so big it almost looks frozen with happiness.

TV and radio announcers swarm Dusty. "How does it feel to win, Dusty?" they ask.

"I would have had a big smile even if I'd come in last," he says. "But it feels great to win."

Because he ran so fast, rumors are flying that Dusty has mistreated his dogs, pushing them too hard. But now, looking at them, everyone knows this isn't true. The dogs are still strong, barking, jumping, and eager to run farther. Dusty has treated them just right. He knows they are his trusted partners—and they're champions.

After taking care of the dogs, Dusty is over-whelmed by exhaustion and hunger. All he wants to do is eat and sleep. He's been running for two days, and now he can barely stand. But he knows that as a good sportsman he should wait for the next racer to come in. Dusty wolfs down a sand-wich, then goes to the race office to check his time. He ran the 158-mile course in fourteen hours and forty-five minutes. His team averaged eleven miles per hour! Over the radio he hears that Andy is approaching the finish. Dusty returns to greet his friend and second-place finisher. Andy finishes, carrying an injured dog in his sled; he's one hour and eighteen minutes behind Dusty.

Dusty leaves with his family for some much-needed sleep. Later that night, they return for the awards banquet, where Dusty is loaded up with prizes. Along with a trophy and many smaller awards, Dusty wins a thousand-dollar college scholarship and two plane tickets to Nome to see the finish of the big Iditarod.

But his favorite prize is a beautiful sled hand-made by one of the most famous mushers in Alaska, Al Marples. To race in this sled next year is a tribute Dusty vows not to miss. As champion, he'll return to defend his title and to teach upcoming mushers the honor of carrying on Alaska's most enduring tradition.